All About Instruments

by Sascha Goddard

OXFORD
UNIVERSITY PRESS
AUSTRALIA & NEW ZEALAND

T0362630

Instruments Make Music

Musical instruments are played all around the world. The sounds instruments make can be very different.

Instruments can be grouped into families, based on how they make sounds.

Musicians can play instruments **solo** or together. In **orchestras** and bands, the different sounds blend to make music.

Orchestras can have between 50 and 100 musicians.

The Woodwind Family

Woodwind instruments are played by blowing air. A musician blows into or over a hole in the instrument, or into a mouthpiece with a **reed** in it. Air moves through the instrument and makes a sound.

reed

Some woodwind instruments
are tiny and others are huge.

Flute

A flute is held in a sideways direction. A musician blows across the mouth hole, while their fingers open and close the keys.

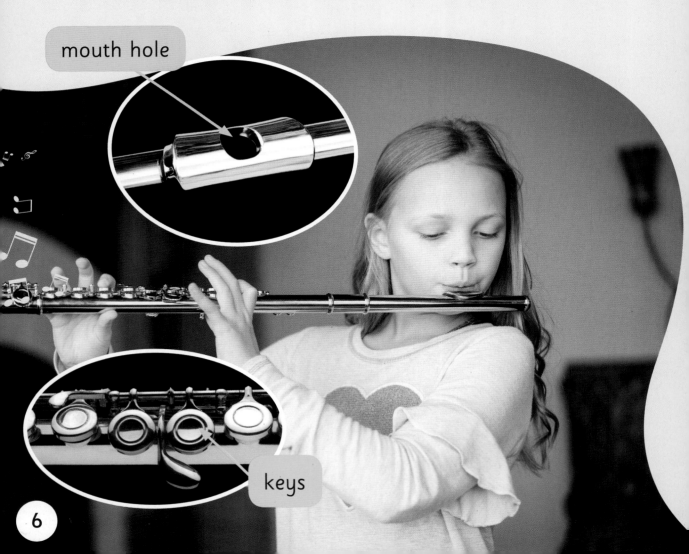

mouth hole

keys

Saxophone

The saxophone can be played sitting or standing. A musician blows into the mouthpiece and touches the keys to make **notes**.

What's that instrument?

The harmonica is played by sucking in air like a vacuum.

Many jazz songs feature a saxophone solo.

The Brass Family

Brass instruments are commonly found in brass bands.

A musician puts their lips together tightly and blows into a mouthpiece. The idea is to make their lips buzz, so air moves through the instrument.

A **valve** or **slide** changes the notes the instrument makes.

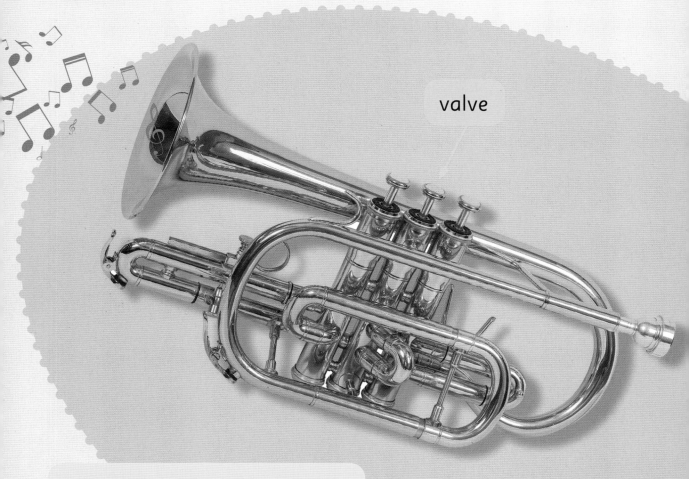

valve

A cornet has a smoother sound than a trumpet.

Trumpet

A trumpet is held straight out in front. A musician touches valves to make different notes.

The trumpet is the oldest brass instrument and makes the highest notes.

Trombone

The trombone has a slide to change the **pitch**. The slide is pushed straight out to make a low sound. It is pulled backwards, towards the musician, to make a higher sound.

slide

mouthpiece

What's that instrument?

A serpent is an instrument that looks a bit like a snake.

It has a cup-shaped mouthpiece.

The String Family

String instruments are plucked, strummed or played with a bow to make sound.

Most string instruments have a hollow section. This means that there is an empty hole inside the instrument. This area helps them make sound, too.

hollow

bow

strings

A string quartet has four musicians.

What's that instrument?

The hurdy-gurdy is a peculiar instrument.
A handle turns a wheel, which rubs
against strings to make sound.

Violin

The violin is the smallest instrument in the string family.

A musician holds it under their chin and plays it with a bow.

chin rest

bow

Banjo

The banjo has a round section called a belly and a long, flat stick called a neck.

A musician strums or plucks the strings with a **pick**.

pick

The Percussion Family

A musician plays percussion instruments by hitting, shaking or scraping them.

Percussion instruments are
different shapes and sizes.

Drum

Drums are hit with drumsticks to keep the beat.

Drums commonly make loud bangs and thuds.
They can make soft sounds, too.

A drummer uses pedals to play some drums.

Triangle

A triangle is a metal bar bent into a triangle shape. It makes a dinging sound when it is hit with a bar.

What's that instrument?

This seed pod shaker comes from Peru.

It makes a rattling sound.

The Voice

Our voices are instruments, too.

The voice is the oldest instrument and is used in many cultures all around the world. The mouth, throat and lungs make this instrument work.

Each singing voice sounds different.

What's that instrument?

A throat singer can make many sounds at the same time.

All Together Now

Instruments make different sounds in different ways.

Family	Instruments	How they make sound
woodwind	flute, saxophone	blowing into or across a hole
brass	trumpet, trombone	buzzing the lips on a mouthpiece
strings	violin, banjo	plucking, strumming or using a bow
percussion	drums, triangle	hitting, shaking or scraping
voice	singing	using the mouth, throat and lungs

Glossary

notes: single sounds in music

orchestras: many musicians playing instruments together

pick: a small tool used to pluck strings on an instrument

pitch: how high or low sounds are in music

reed: a thin strip of material that makes the sound in wind instruments

slide: part of an instrument that slides backwards and forwards to change the note

solo: on their own

valve: part of an instrument that opens and closes to change the note

Index